I *love* YOU BECAUSE...

I love YOU BECAUSE...

QUESTIONS & ANSWERS TO SHARE WITH THE ONE YOU LOVE

JULIE DAY

Castle Point Books
New York

I LOVE YOU BECAUSE. Copyright © 2018 by St. Martin's Press.
All rights reserved.
Printed in the United States of America.
For information, address St. Martin's Press,
175 Fifth Avenue, New York, N.Y. 10010.

www.stmartins.com
www.castlepointbooks.com

The Castle Point Books trademark is owned by Castle Point Publishing, LLC.
Castle Point books are published and distributed by St. Martin's Press.

ISBN 978-1-250-20227-7 (trade paperback)

Our books may be purchased in bulk for promotional, educational, or business
use. Please contact your local bookseller or the Macmillan Corporate and
Premium Sales Department at 1-800-221-7945, extension 5442, or by email at
MacmillanSpecialMarkets@macmillan.com.

First Edition: December 2018

10 9 8 7 6 5 4 3 2 1

This book is for:

....

EVERY LOVE STORY
IS
beautiful,
BUT OURS IS
MY
favorite.

Contents

Introduction

Saying those three little words isn't always easy. This question-and-answer journal does the work for you, making it simple and fun to communicate with the one you love. Through quizzes and queries ranging from playful and funny to sweet and serious, you can share all the deepest emotions you have been longing to express and connect in ways you never knew you could before.

Approach the questions with an open heart—track down your answers, think them through, and discover what makes your love so special. When the journal is complete, you'll have a modern-day, loving ode to your relationship. Share this with your partner to open the door to better communication, loving expression, and fuller hearts. Embolden your relationship by saying, *I Love You Because...*

HOW YOU

1. When we first met, you made my heart skip a beat when:

_____

2. I find you most attractive when:

_____

_____

_____

3. You make me feel:

a) confident

b) sexy

c) loved

d) appreciated

4. When I am at my lowest, you always

_____

_____ to make me smile.

5. We balance each other out most when:

_____

6. You show your appreciation through:
a) words
b) gifts
c) grand gestures
d) helpful efforts

7. I feel like the center of the universe whenever you:

_____

_____

8. You always know how to make me laugh by:

_____

_____

9. You are the _____ to my

_____.

10. I can't stop smiling when you:

_____

_____

11. The words I love to hear most from you:

_____

12. If I could imagine a perfect day with you, it would include:

_____

_____

13. It makes me feel _____ when I see

you _____.

14. I feel most loved when you:

a) wrap your arms around me

b) lend a helping hand

c) tell me you love me

d) listen to me

15. I love how your eyes light up when:

_____

_____

16. If you were a character from an epic romance, you would be:

_____

_____

17. The sound of your laugh makes me feel:

_____

_____

18. *I love it when you:*

a) tickle me

b) cuddle me

c) massage me

d) caress me

19. *The nickname you have for me that makes my heart flutter:*

_____

_____

20. *When you touch me, I feel:*

_____

_____

21. *When I am distant, you pull me back by:*

_____

_____

22. I knew I was in love with you when:

_____

_____

_____

_____

23. When I hear the song _____
_____, I think of you.

24. You fill me with love when:

_____

_____

_____

_____

25. Your love is like _____,
and I never want that to change.

26. When you gaze at me, my first thought is:

_____

_____

27. When you reach for me, I feel:

_____

_____

28. I know you will always make me feel:

a) safe

b) loved

c) desired

d) appreciated

29. I feel giddy when:

_____

_____

_____

30. Our perfect evening would include:

a) dancing

b) dinner for two

c) a comfy spot on the couch

d) a place only we know

31. When I am cold, you:

_____

_____

32. Your voice calms me down when:

_____

_____

_____

33. I get goosebumps when you:

_____

_____

34. One thing you do that makes me feel loved:

_____

_____

_____

_____

35. I am so lucky that you always _____

_____ for me.

36. I feel most appreciated when:

_____

_____

_____

37. I am grateful you never _____

_____.

38. You are not like other partners because:

_____

_____

39. You are the only one who has ever:

_____

_____

40. I know you love me because:

_____

_____

41. If your love were expressed in nature, it would be:

a) a soaring eagle

b) a rushing river

c) an erupting volcano

d) a blooming flower

42. You keep me safe by:

a) wrapping your arms around me

b) taking my hand

c) never letting me out of your sight

d) letting me have my space

43. In our most intimate moments, you make me feel like _____ from the movies.

44. You make me feel like I mean everything to you by:

_____

_____

45. You always know how to touch me, especially:

_____

_____

46. The best surprise you have ever given me was:

_____

_____

47. It always cheers me up when you:

_____

_____

48. If your love were a ride at a theme park, it would be:

_____

_____

49. I go wild when you:

_____

_____

50. *I knew you loved me when:*

_____

_____

51. *I feel at home with you when you:*

a) make me laugh

b) hold me

c) tell me you love me

d) fall asleep next to me

52. *If your love were a physical object, it would be:*

_____

_____

53. *I love how you love me because:*

_____

_____

THE
Little Things

1. Your physical features that make me feel weak in the knees:

_____

_____

2. My favorite quirk of yours:

_____

_____

_____

3. _____ is the word I would use to describe you.

4. My favorite silly expression that you make:

_____

_____

_____

5. You think _____ is an imperfection, but I think it's _____.

6. I love the way you _____ when you smile.

7. I felt a thrill the first time you:

_____

_____

_____

_____

8. My favorite freckle, scar, or dimple on your body:

_____

_____

_____

9. If you were a drink, you would be:

_____

_____

10. A habit of yours that makes me smile:

_____

_____

_____

11. You look best when you wear:

_____

_____

_____

12. My favorite place to touch you:

_____

_____

13. I love the sound you make when you:

_____

_____

14. Your love is like magic when you:

_____

_____

15. The funniest thing you have ever said to me:

_____

_____

_____

16. An awkward moment that I love:

_____

_____

_____

17. When I think of you, I think of:

_____

_____

_____

_____

18. You are cuter than:

_____

19. If you were a sweet treat, you would be:

_____

20. You have the best reactions when:

_____

_____

_____

_____

21. One thing you do better than anyone else:

_____

_____

22. The song lyrics that remind me of you:

_____

_____

_____

23. The places that remind me of you:

_____

_____

24. The times you look the happiest:

_____

_____

_____

25. If you lived in another time period, it would be:

_____

_____

26. I love how you look when you watch me:

_____

_____

_____

27. The best thing you have taught me:

_____

_____

_____

28. You are the _____ person I have ever met.

29. You look invincible when:

_____

_____

_____

_____

_____

30. _____ is your look-alike.

31. I laugh the hardest when you:

_____

_____

_____

_____

32. Your way of _____

_____ makes my heart melt.

33. *Your personality is:*

a) relaxed like the breeze

b) salty like the sea

c) steady like the earth

d) bright like lightning

34. *You are most confident when:*

_____

_____

35. *What you have that other people lack:*

_____

_____

36. *If you were in a movie, you would be this kind of character:*

_____

_____

37. Your _____ is infectious.

38. _____ may not be your strong suit, but _____ sure is.

39. I think it's adorable when you:

_____

_____

_____

_____

40. I used to find _____ unappealing, but I changed my mind when I saw you.

41. If you were a season, you would be:

_____

42. One time, while you weren't looking:

_____

_____

_____

_____

43. I love your:

a) smell

b) taste

c) appearance

d) touch

44. If I could keep one thing about you all to myself, it would be:

_____

_____

_____

_____

45. I could stare at your _____ forever.

46. When I see _____, I think of you.

47. I don't even mind your:

_____

_____

_____

_____

48. When you are old and gray, I imagine:

_____

_____

_____

_____

_____

49. *Your love is:*

a) an extreme sport
b) a soothing caress
c) a revving engine
d) a winding river

50. *Your way of* _____ *turns me on.*

51. _____ *is your most attractive quality.*

52. *I chose you because:*

_____

_____

_____

_____

_____

HOW YOU
Build Me Up

1. I feel supported when you:

_____

_____

2. When I am with you, I can be myself because:

_____

_____

3. Even when I am a mess, you make me feel:

a) beautiful

b) even-keeled

c) adored

d) normal

4. You make me a better person when you:

_____

_____

5. You put up with my _____
even when _____.

6. When I am feeling down, you always:

_____
_____
_____

7. You make me feel successful because:

_____
_____
_____

8. If we were a sports team, we would be called:

_____
_____

9. Even when we are in a fight, you always _____ to let me know you care.

10. You would never:

_____

_____

_____

11. You would let me win at:

_____

_____

_____

12. If I got arrested, you would:

a) bail me out

b) let me sit overnight

c) visit me

d) sit in the cell next to me

13. In my toughest moments, you:

_____

_____

14. When the road gets rough, you always tell me this to make me feel better:

_____

_____

15. If you have to choose between me and _____, you would choose:

_____

16. When I watch you _____ with our _____, I know:

_____

_____

17. The biggest challenge we have faced together:

_____

_____

_____

18. My world is better when you:

_____

_____

19. When I think of how you support me,
I am reminded of:

_____

_____

20. You fiercely defended me when:

_____

_____

21. You always let me have the last:

_____

_____

22. You would never _____ to hurt me.

23. When I am feeling uncertain, you:

_____

_____

_____

24. When I second-guess myself, this makes me feel better:

_____

_____

_____

25. My favorite line from a move or show that reminds me of your love:

_____

_____

26. If you were a famous structure of support, you would be:

a) the Golden Gate Bridge

b) the Arc de Triomphe

c) the Hoover Dam

d) the Leaning Tower of Pisa

27. When I am feeling wounded, you:

_____

28. Instead of a bandage, you heal my hurts with:

_____

29. When you say you are sorry, you make things better by:

_____

_____

30. When I feel insecure about _____, you lift me up this way:

_____

_____

31. You love me more than:

_____

32. We are partners in:

a) crime

b) life

c) love

d) lust

33. You make the simple things, like _____ _____ happy.

34. When I lost my _____, you made it all okay.

35. The best advice you have ever given me:

_____

_____

_____

_____

36. When you are being silly, you always:

_____

_____

_____

_____

37. If my feelings were a house of cards, this is how you would make sure they don't fall:

_____

_____

38. The best small gesture you make when I am feeling sad:

_____

39. When you can't put something into words, this is what you do:

_____

40. One time I didn't think I deserved your help, but you were there anyway:

_____

_____

41. You make me feel like a million:

_____

_____

42. The biggest gesture you have ever made to make me feel happy:

_____

_____

_____

43. You put yourself on the line for me when you:

_____

_____

44. When I pick apart my _____, you put it back together.

45. You bring out the best in me when:

_____

_____

_____

46. You have always supported _____

_____, even when I thought it was

not possible.

47. You raise my spirits when:

_____

_____

48. Even when I am mad, you get me to crack

a smile by:

_____

_____

49. If I fall apart, you put me back together with:

_____

_____

50. You give me just what I need every time you:

_____

_____

51. Your encouragement feels like:

_____

_____

52. If one thing is unconditional, it's:

_____

_____

YOUR
Greatest
Strengths

1. I am mesmerized by the way you:

_____

_____

_____

2. Your secret talent that I love:

_____

_____

3. The way your mind works is like a:

_____

_____

4. In your professional life, I am most proud of:

a) your work ethic

b) your ability to provide

c) your drive

d) your education

5. Your interest in _____
inspires me to:

_____

_____

6. What I admire about you most is:

_____

_____

7. If I could have one of your strengths,
it would be:

_____

_____

8. You light up most when:

_____

_____

9. I love when you get fired up about:

_____

_____

10. I love your philosophy on life because:

_____

_____

11. It makes me happy that your core values include:

_____

_____

_____

12. Your biggest priorities are:

_____

_____

13. Of all your skills, this one is my favorite:

_____

_____

14. You should give yourself more credit for:

_____

_____

15. You may not see it, but you are amazing at:

_____

_____

16. You make the most out of a bad situation when:

_____

_____

_____

17. *Of all your interests, I love that you love:*

_____

_____

18. *I am inspired by how passionate you are about:*

_____

_____

19. *You come alive when:*

_____

_____

_____

20. *Your biggest thrill is my biggest:*

_____

_____

21. You never make a big deal about:

_____

_____

22. It makes me feel great that you care so much about:

_____

_____

23. Even after a long day at work, you still:

_____

_____

24. You always remember:

_____

_____

_____

25. *You personify:*

a) honesty

b) loyalty

c) trustworthiness

d) integrity

26. *You show that value best by:*

_____

_____

_____

27. *You make other people happy when you:*

_____

_____

_____

28. *Your family means* _____

_____ *to you:*

29. You are a true friend to:

_____

30. You show you care for others best by:

_____

_____

_____

31. You are most selfless when it comes to:

_____

_____

_____

32. Your values are strongest in this regard:

_____

_____

_____

33. *You express your values in this way:*

_____

_____

34. *Your acts of service to others include:*

_____

_____

_____

35. *You are an example to others in the way you:*

_____

_____

36. *You will always stand up for others when:*

_____

_____

37. You put _____ ahead of yourself when:

_____

_____

38. Little things you do for others that not everyone sees:

_____

_____

39. You make the world better by:

_____

_____

40. Other people wish they had your:

_____

_____

41. If all your friends had one way to describe you, it would be:

_____

_____

42. If you made the 6 o'clock news, it would be for:

_____

_____

43. Your silliest trait that makes everyone smile:

_____

_____

44. You are best known for your:

_____

_____

45. You deserve more recognition for:

_____

_____

_____

46. You should be most proud of:

_____

_____

_____

47. I am most grateful for the way you:

_____

_____

_____

48. _____ appreciate you most for your _____.

49. You are the most loving when it comes to:

_____

_____

50. When we are alone, you make me feel loved by:

_____

_____

51. The world falls away when you:

_____

_____

52. In our romantic moments, you are best at:

_____

_____

_____

53. Your signature move that I love the most:

_____

_____

54. You shine when you:

_____

_____

55. Somehow, you read my mind when:

_____

_____

56. Your greatest quirks and qualities, in sum:

a) _____

b) _____

c) _____

d) _____

57. The very first moments I spent with you, I could tell:

_____

_____

58. At the same time, I wanted to know these things about you:

_____

_____

59. I fall more deeply in love with you every time you:

_____

_____

60. I only hope that I can return all the
_____ you give me.

The Love
WE SHARE

1. I love our love because:

_____

_____

_____

2. If I couldn't tell you I love you with words, I would:

_____

_____

3. If I could give you anything:

_____

_____

4. Our love story is most like that of:

_____

_____

5. My favorite activity that we do as a couple:

_____

_____

6. The thing I love most about our relationship:

_____

_____

_____

7. I think we are the funniest when:

_____

_____

8. We have the most fun when:

_____

_____

9. We would win a relationship award for our:

_____

10. We are the best team when it comes to:

_____

_____

_____

11. Other couples envy our:

_____

_____

_____

12. We are a balancing act with:

_____

_____

_____

13. On our first date, I knew I wanted a second one when:

_____

14. Our personal strengths complement one another in this way:

_____

_____

15. If we were a Venn diagram, the middle would say:

_____

16. If we were on a trivia team, we would:

a) come in last place

b) butt heads

c) work together pretty well

d) be reigning champions

17. We give each other independence by:

_____

_____

18. We are dependent on each other for:

_____

_____

19. When we are together in public, we are:

a) inseparable

b) affectionate

c) loving from a distance

d) comfortable with space

20. I love that we support each other best when it comes to:

_____

_____

21. A challenge we have overcome as a couple:

_____

_____

22. We face difficulties best by:

_____

_____

23. We offer each other healthy challenges in this way:

_____

_____

_____

24. We have high expectations for our:

_____

_____

25. Our chemistry is:

a) an ocean tide

b) a raging fire

c) a roller coaster

d) a quiet meadow

26. Our physical connection is most passionate when it comes to:

_____

_____

27. Our love feels the most intense when:

_____

_____

28. Our love is the steadiest when:

_____

_____

29. Our best day together was:

_____

_____

30. If I had to sum our relationship up in a quote, lyric, or one-liner, it would be:

_____

_____

31. My favorite part of my day with you:

_____

32. If there is just one _____ left, we will:

a) share it

b) play tug-of-war

c) let the other person have it

d) have something else

33. The cornerstone of our relationship is:

_____

_____

34. What makes us a success is:

_____

_____

35. Even when we disagree, we can always come back to:

_____

_____

36. It gives me hope that we always:

_____

_____

_____

37. When one of us is going through a hard time, we:

_____

_____

38. I love our friendship because:

_____

_____

39. What we give each other that other friends can't:

_____

_____

40. Little surprises that make all the difference:

_____

_____

41. We celebrate each other's successes by:

_____

_____

42. We have each other's backs when:

_____

_____

43. We always have good luck when it comes to:

_____

_____

44. We really connect on:

_____

_____

45. We don't share these interests, but you support my _____ as much as I support your:

_____

46. Even though we have conflicting feelings on _____, it still works because:

_____

_____

47. Our puzzle pieces fit best in this regard:

_____

_____

48. Our biggest achievement as a couple:

_____

_____

49. Our rainbow after a storm is:

_____

_____

50. Even through hard times, our love is worth it because:

_____

_____

51. If our love were a famous work of art, it would be:

_____

_____

52. Our relationship fills my heart because:

_____

_____

THE LOVE
Ahead

1. When I think about tomorrow with you, I am:

_____

_____

2. When I think about 10 years from now, I imagine:

_____

_____

_____

3. I am most excited about this little thing on our calendar:

_____

_____

4. I will always look forward to _____
_____ with you.

5. Your approach to _____ makes me excited for the future.

6. Your drive to always _____ _____ makes me feel confident.

7. I love the idea of _____ _____ _____ as we get older.

8. The way you _____ _____ will only make our relationship stronger.

9. To express my love better, I will:

_____

10. Something you give to me that I hope never ends:

_____

_____

_____

_____

11. I will always love how you:

_____

_____

_____

_____

12. I will learn to love:

_____

_____

_____

13. I love the idea of _____

_____ with you some day.

14. From the first day I met you, you have always:

_____

_____

_____

15. I hope you will never stop:

_____

_____

_____

16. Your love remains a constant source of:

_____

_____

17. My biggest hope for the days ahead:

_____

_____

_____

18. I hope we show each other love more by:

_____

_____

_____

19. Your presence today makes my tomorrow look:

_____

_____

20. You will be my _____ and my _____ for years to come.

21. When I dream of what our love will be like down the road, I imagine:

_____

_____

22. Your hopes and aspirations mesh with mine in this way:

_____

_____

23. I will never _____, and only _____ so you will always feel loved.

24. When I think of where our love will go, I think of these things:

_____

25. I know I will love the way you _____
_____ forever.

26. When I think of loving you, my heart:

_____

_____

27. The sun will rise and set with your:

_____

_____

28. I am most grateful for these opportunities for us ahead:

_____

_____

_____

_____

10 THINGS
I Love About You:

1. _____

_____

2. _____

_____

3. _____

_____

4. _____

_____

5. _____

_____

6. _____

_____

7. _____

_____

8. _____

_____

9. _____

_____

10. _____

_____

10 PROMISES
I Will Make to You:

1. _____

   _____

2. _____

   _____

3. _____

   _____

4. _____

   _____

5. _____

_____

6. _____

_____

7. _____

_____

8. _____

_____

9. _____

_____

10. _____

_____

Dear _____,

I love you because...

_____

_____

_____

_____

_____

_____

_____

_____

_____

_____

_____

_____

_____

_____

_____
_____
_____
_____
_____
_____
_____
_____
_____
_____
_____
_____
_____
_____
_____

Love _____

&

{place photo here}